PIANO · VOCAL · GUITAR

STILL MORE SONGS OF THE FIFTIES

THE DECADE SERIES

M000104888

Contents

ISBN 0-7935-4429-7

HAL·LEONARD®
CORPORATION

7777 W. BLUEMOUND RD. P.O. BOX 13819 MILWAUKEE, WI 53213

Visit Hal Leonard Online at
www.halleonard.com

AUTUMN LEAVES

English lyric by JOHNNY MERCER
French lyric by JACQUES PREVERT
Music by JOSEPH KOSMA

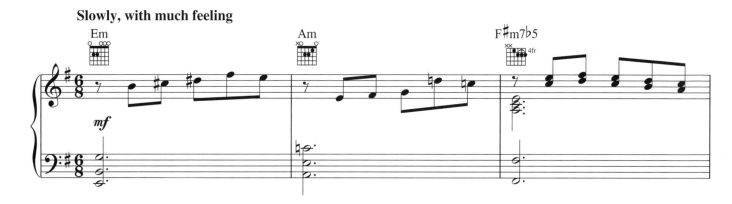

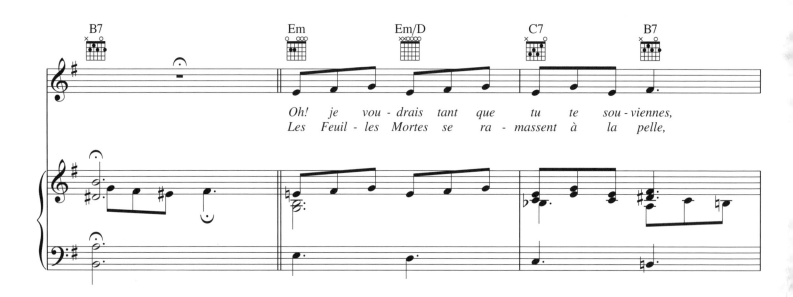

Oh! je vou - drais tant que tu te sou - viennes,
Les Feuil - les Mortes se ra - massent à la pelle,

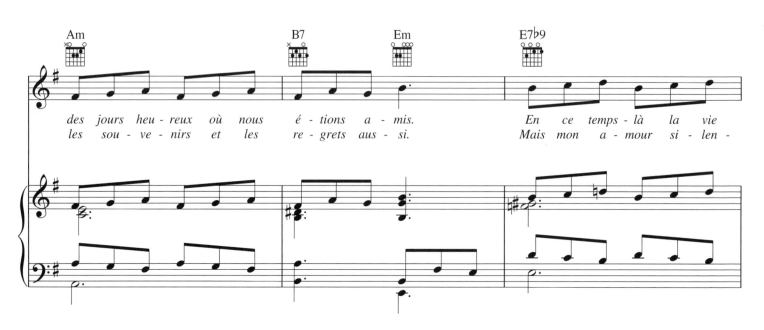

des jours heu - reux où nous é - tions a - mis.
les sou - ve - nirs et les re - grets aus - si.

En ce temps - là la vie
Mais mon a - mour si - len -

BAUBLES, BANGLES AND BEADS

from KISMET

Words and Music by ROBERT WRIGHT
and GEORGE FORREST
(Music Based on Themes of A. BORODIN)

CHANTILLY LACE

Words and Music by
J.P. RICHARDSON

A BIG HUNK O' LOVE

Words and Music by AARON SCHROEDER
and SID WYCHE

Bright Rock

Hey, ba - by! ___

I ain't ask - in' much of you. No no no no no no no no,

ba - by, I ain't ask - in' much of you.

COUNT YOUR BLESSINGS INSTEAD OF SHEEP

from the Motion Picture Irving Berlin's WHITE CHRISTMAS

Words and Music by
IRVING BERLIN

CATCH A FALLING STAR

Words and Music by PAUL VANCE
and LEE POCKRISS

COLD, COLD HEART

Words and Music by
HANK WILLIAMS

Lyrics: I've tried so hard, my dear, to show that you're my ev'ry dream,

There was a time when I be-lieved _ that you be-longed _ to me, _____ but now I know your heart is shack-led to a ___ mem - o - ry. _____ The more I learn to

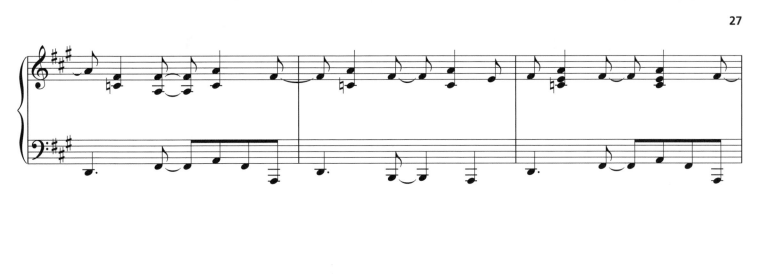

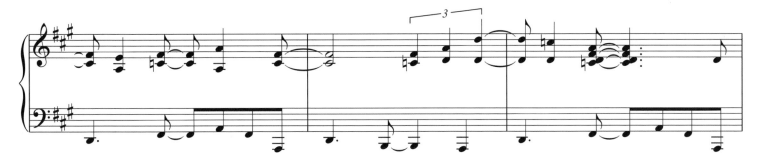

DANCE WITH ME HENRY
(The Wallflower)

Words and Music by HANK BALLARD,
ETTA JAMES and JOHNNY OTIS

Hey, ba - by, what do I have to do ___ to

make you love me too? ___ You got to roll with me, Hen - ry.
Roll with me, Hen - ry. (Al -

- right, ba - by) Roll ___ with me, Hen - ry. (Don't ___ mean may - be)

DON'T

Words and Music by JERRY LEIBER
and MIKE STOLLER

DON'T LET THE STARS GET IN YOUR EYES

Words and Music by
SLIM WILLET

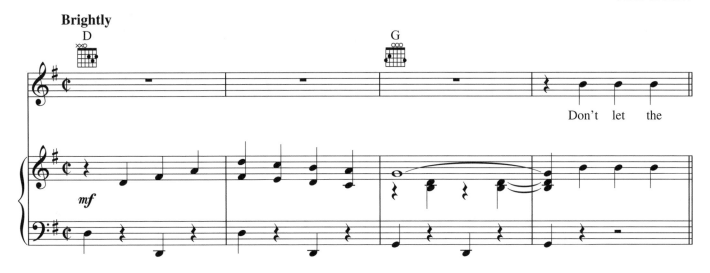

Brightly

Don't let the

stars get in your eyes, don't let the moon break your heart. _____

Love blooms at night, in day-light it

GET A JOB

Words and Music by EARL BEAL, RICHARD LEWIS,
RAYMOND EDWARDS and WILLIAM HORTON

43

HEARTACHES BY THE NUMBER

Words and Music by
HARLAN HOWARD

(Now and Then There's)
A FOOL SUCH AS I

Words and Music by
BILL TRADER

HOW IMPORTANT CAN IT BE?

By BENNIE BENJAMIN
and GEORGE WEISS

I BEG OF YOU

Words and Music by ROSE MARIE McCOY
and KELLY OWENS

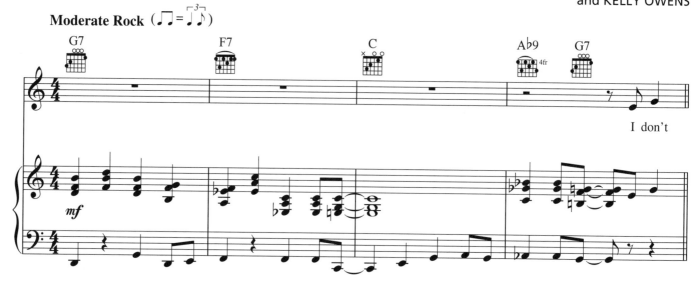

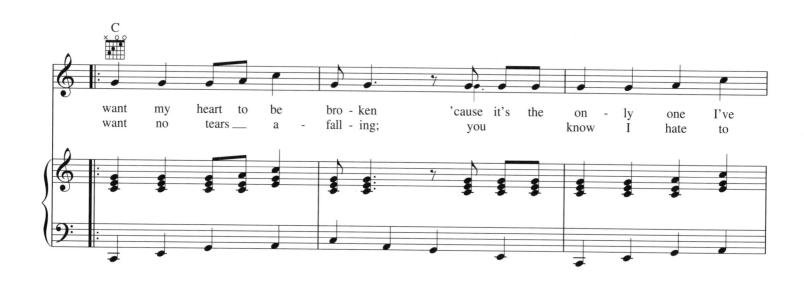

I DON'T CARE IF
THE SUN DON'T SHINE

Words and Music by
MACK DAVID

('Til)
I KISSED YOU

Words and Music by
DON EVERLY

Nev - er felt like this __ un - til I kissed you.
Things have real - ly changed __ since I kissed you.

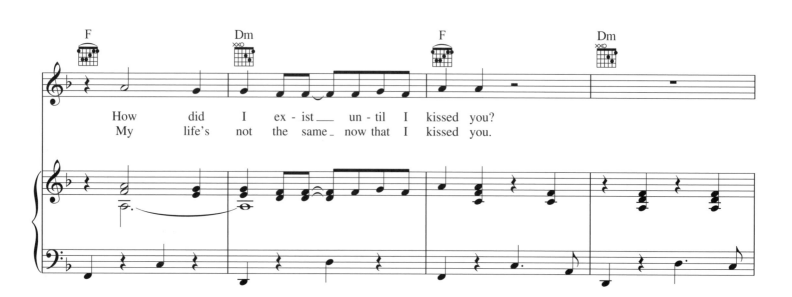

How did I ex - ist __ un - til I kissed you?
My life's not the same __ now that I kissed you.

IT'S NOT FOR ME TO SAY

Words by AL STILLMAN
Music by ROBERT ALLEN

I'LL BE HOME

Words and Music by FERDINAND WASHINGTON
and STAN LEWIS

JUST A DREAM

Words and Music by
BIG BILL BROONZY

JAILHOUSE ROCK
from JAILHOUSE ROCK

Words and Music by JERRY LEIBER
and MIKE STOLLER

1. The war-den threw a par-ty in the
2.-5. *(See additional lyrics)*

coun-ty jail.___ The pris-on band was there and they be-

gan to wail.___ The band was jump-in' and the joint be-

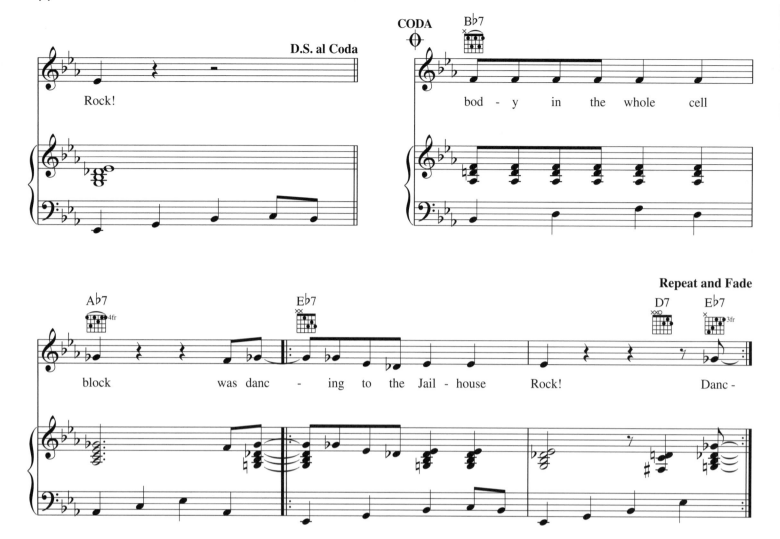

Additional Lyrics

2. Spider Murphy played the tenor saxophone
   Little Joe was blowin' on the slide trombone.
   The drummer boy from Illinois went crash, boom, bang;
   The whole rhythm section was the Purple Gang.
   Chorus

3. Number Forty-seven said to number Three,
   "You're the cutest jailbird I ever did see.
   I sure would be delighted with your company,
   Come on and do the Jailhouse Rock with me."
   Chorus

4. The sad sack was a-sittin' on a block of stone,
   Way over in the corner weeping all alone.
   The warden said, "Hey, Buddy, don't you be no square,
   If you can't find a partner, use a wooden chair!"
   Chorus

5. Shifty Henry said to Bugs, "For heaven's sake,
   No one's lookin', now's our chance to make a break."
   Bugsy turned to Shifty and he said, "Nix, nix;
   I wanna stick around a while and get my kicks."
   Chorus

LONELY STREET

Words and Music by CARL BELEW,
W.S. STEVENSON and KENNY SOWDER

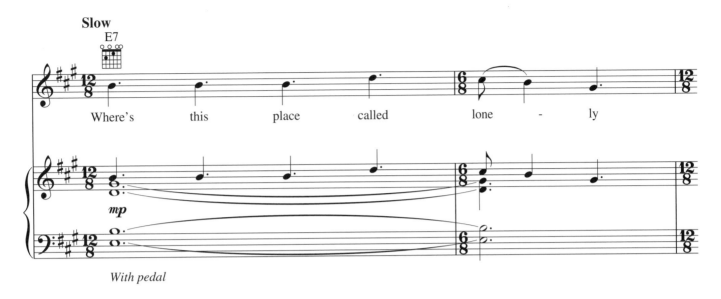

Where's this place called lone - ly

With pedal

street? _____ I'm

look - ing _____ for that lone - ly street;
A place where there's _____ just lone - li - ness;

LIPSTICK ON YOUR COLLAR

Moderate rock beat

Words by EDNA LEWIS
Music by GEORGE GOEHRING

MEMORIES ARE MADE OF THIS

Words and Music by RICHARD DEHR,
FRANK MILLER and TERRY GILKYSON

MARIANNE
(All Day, All Night, Marianne)

By TERRY GILKYSON,
RICHARD DEHR and FRANK MILLER

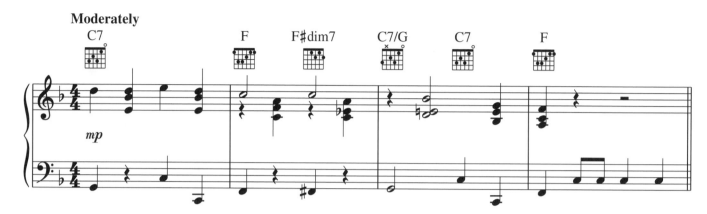

Mar - i - anne, oh, Mar - i - anne, oh, won't you mar - ry me?
When she walks a - long the shore, peo - ple pause to greet.
When we mar - ry we will have a time you nev - er saw.

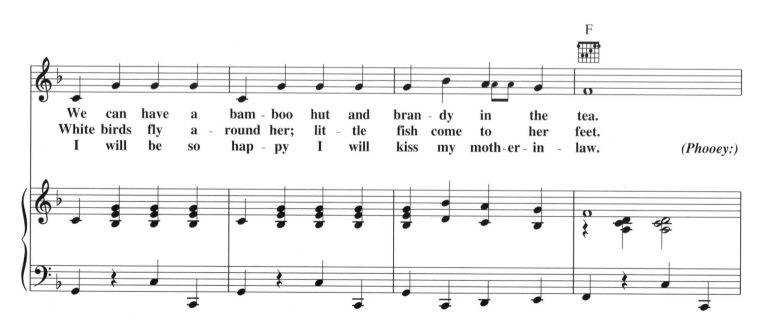

We can have a bam - boo hut and bran - dy in the tea.
White birds fly a - round her; lit - tle fish come to her feet.
I will be so hap - py I will kiss my moth - er - in - law.

(Phooey:)

MISTER SANDMAN

Lyric and Music by
PAT BALLARD

MOMENTS TO REMEMBER

Words by AL STILLMAN
Music by ROBERT ALLEN

MY PRAYER

Music by GEORGES BOULANGER
Lyric and Musical Adaptation by JIMMY KENNEDY

Moderately slow

When the twi-light is gone ___ and no song bird is sing - ing, ___

___ When the twi-light is gone ___ you come in - to my

OH! CAROL

Words and Music by HOWARD GREENFIELD
and NEIL SEDAKA

NO, NOT MUCH!

Words by AL STILLMAN
Music by ROBERT ALLEN

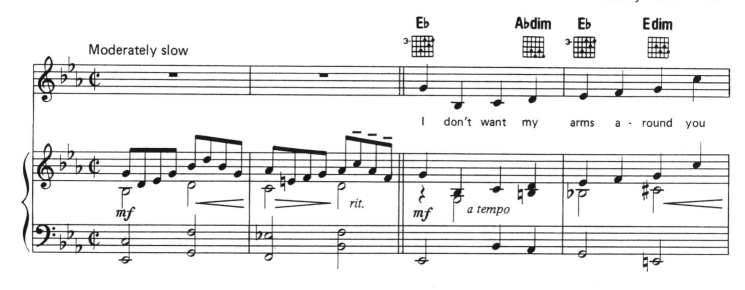

Moderately slow

I don't want my arms a-round you

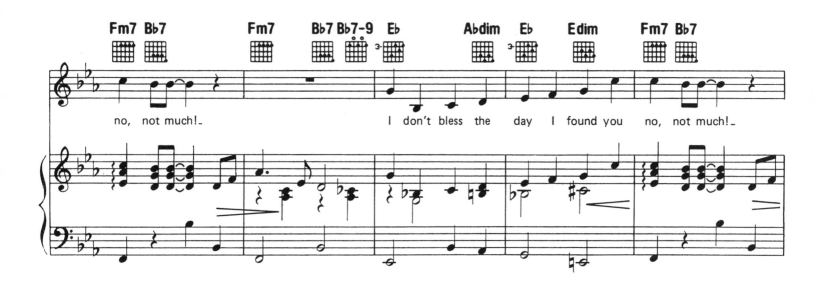

no, not much!_ I don't bless the day I found you no, not much!_

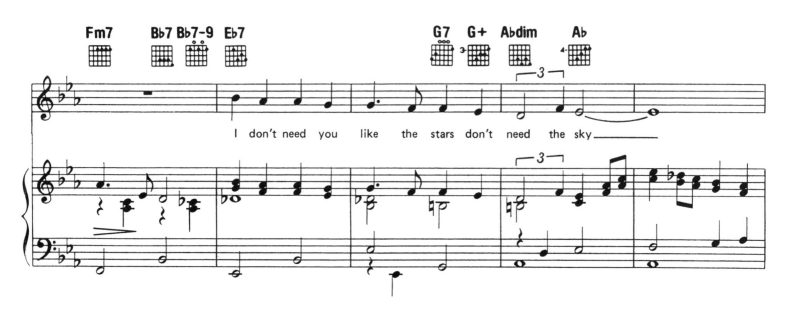

I don't need you like the stars don't need the sky_____

PEGGY SUE

Words and Music by JERRY ALLISON,
NORMAN PETTY and BUDDY HOLLY

PROBLEMS

Words and Music by BOUDLEAUX BRYANT
and FELICE BRYANT

Prob - lems, prob - lems, prob - lems all day long.
Wor - ries, wor - ies pile up on my head.

Will my prob - lems work out right or
Woe is me; ___ I should have stayed in

wrong?   My ba - by don't like ___
bed.   Can't get the car; my ___

*Recorded a half step lower.

113

SEARCHIN'

Words and Music by JERRY LEIBER
and MIKE STOLLER

Not too fast, with a strong afterbeat

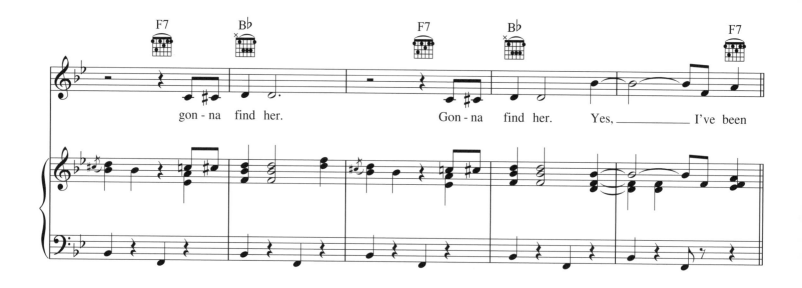

SIDE BY SIDE

Words and Music by
HARRY WOODS

SINCE I MET YOU BABY

Words and Music by
IVORY JOE HUNTER

Slow Blues

Refrain

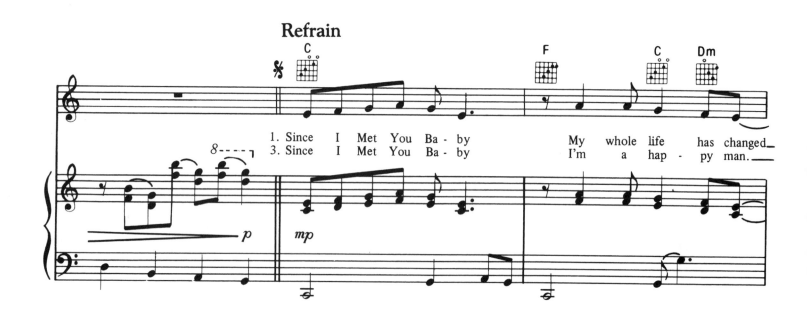

1. Since I Met You Ba - by   My whole life has changed
3. Since I Met You Ba - by   I'm a hap - py man.

SIXTEEN CANDLES

Words and Music by LUTHER DIXON
and ALLYSON R. KHENT

SKOKIAAN
(South African Song)

Words by TOM GLAZER
Music by AUGUST MSARURGWA

be-side a jun-gle bun-ga-low. _____ The

hot drums ___ are drum-min', ___ the hot strings ___ are

strum-min', ___ and warm lips ___ are bliss-ful, ___ they're

kiss-full ___ of sko-ki-aan. ___ Ho, ho, _____

SPLISH SPLASH

Words and Music by BOBBY DARIN
and MURRAY KAUFMAN

how was I to know there was a par-ty go-ing on?
went and put my danc-ing shoes __

on. I was a-splish-in' and a-splash-in',
I was a-

roll-in' and a-stroll-in'. I was a-mov-in' and a-groov-in',

Repeat and Fade   **Optional Ending**

I was a-reel-in' with the feel-in'. I was a-

STANDING ON THE CORNER

from THE MOST HAPPY FELLA

By FRANK LOESSER

HERMAN and BOYS:

Stand - ing on the cor - ner watch - ing all the girls go by,
Stand - ing on the cor - ner watch - ing all the girls go by,
Stand - ing on the cor - ner watch - ing all the girls go by,

Stand - ing on the cor - ner watch - ing all the girls go
Stand - ing on the cor - ner giv - ing all the girls the
Stand - ing on the cor - ner un - der - neath a spring - time

by
eye
sky

Broth-er you don't know a nic - er oc - cu -
Broth-er if you've got a rich i - mag - i -
Broth-er you can't go to jail for what you're

STRANGER IN PARADISE

from KISMET

Words and Music by ROBERT WRIGHT
and GEORGE FORREST
(Music Based on Themes of A. Borodin)

STUPID CUPID

Words and Music by HOWARD GREENFIELD
and NEIL SEDAKA

Stu - pid Cu - pid, you're a real mean guy, __ I'd like to clip your wings so

you can't fly. __ I'm in love and it's a cry - in' shame, __

and I know that you're the one to blame. __ Hey, hey,

TEARS ON MY PILLOW

Words and Music by SYLVESTER BRADFORD
and AL LEWIS

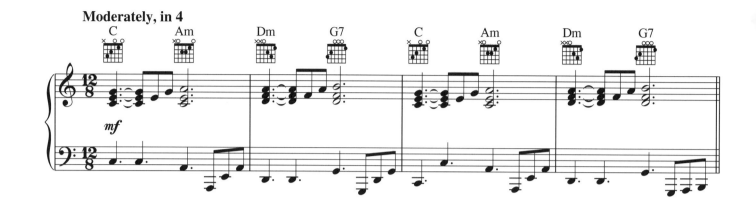

You don't re-mem-ber me, ___ but I re-mem-ber you. ___

'Twas not so long a-go ___ you broke my heart in two. ___

A TEAR FELL

Words and Music by DORIAN BURTON
and EUGENE RANDOLPH

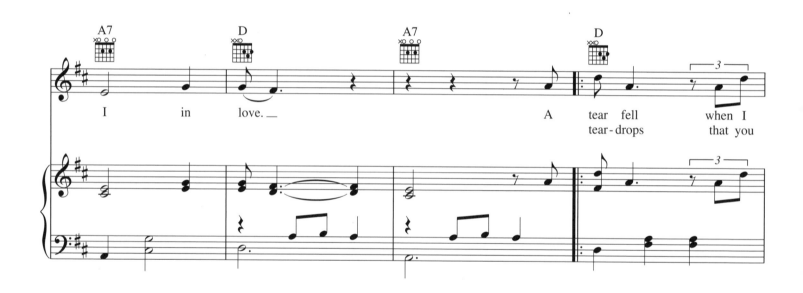

TENNESSEE WALTZ

Words and Music by REDD STEWART
and PEE WEE KING

THERE GOES MY BABY

Words and Music by JERRY LEIBER,
MIKE STOLLER, BEN E. NELSON,
LOVER PATTERSON and GEORGE TREADWELL

TONIGHT YOU BELONG TO ME

Words by BILLY ROSE
Music by LEE DAVID

TWILIGHT TIME

Lyric by BUCK RAM
Music by MORTY NEVINS and AL NEVINS

VENUS

Words and Music by
EDWARD MARSHALL

Hey, Ve - nus, _____ oh, Ve - nus.

Hey, Ve - nus,

Ve - nus, if you will, please send a lit - tle girl for me to thrill,

UNCHAINED MELODY

from the Motion Picture UNCHAINED

Lyric by HY ZARET
Music by ALEX NORTH

WATERLOO

Words and Music by JOHN LOUDERMILK
and MARIJOHN WILKINS

YOUNG LOVE

Words and Music by
RIC CARTEY

WHY DO FOOLS FALL IN LOVE

Words and Music by MORRIS LEVY
and FRANKIE LYMON